WINNIE-THE-POOH

From the stories of A. A. Milne

Dramatized
by
KRISTIN SERGEL

The Dramatic Publishing Company
Woodstock, Illinois • London, England • Melbourne, Australia

*** NOTICE ***

WINNIE-THE-POOH

A Play in Two Acts
For Thirteen Characters

CHARACTERS

CHRISTOPHER ROBIN .... a young boy
WINNIE-THE-POOH .... a teddy bear
PIGLET
OWL
EEYORE .... a donkey
KANGA .... a mother kangaroo
ROO .... her child
RABBIT
ANIMAL 1 .... a small rabbit
ANIMAL 2 *Aurora* .... a small skunk
ANIMAL 3 - *Kendra* .... a rabbit
ANIMAL 4 - *Jessy* .... a rabbit
VOICE .... the narrator

EXTRAS *(other residents of the forest) may be added*

ACT ONE

BEFORE RISE: *CHRISTOPHER ROBIN enters in front of the curtain DR. He is pulling a teddy bear along by one paw, heading for a hassock placed DR.*

CHRISTOPHER ROBIN *(to the bear in a matter-of-fact way).* What would you like to do this evening? Play a game of some sort? *(After looking closely for a response, CHRISTOPHER ROBIN sits down. He speaks toward the audience.)* Winnie-the-Pooh doesn't feel like playing a game. He wants to sit quietly and—*(Looks at the bear again, then up.)* What about a story?

VOICE *(narrator, offstage).* *What* about a story?

CHRISTOPHER ROBIN. Couldn't you very kindly tell him one? Please?

VOICE *(after a slight pause).* What sort of story does he like?

CHRISTOPHER ROBIN *(eagerly).* About himself. He's that sort of bear.

VOICE. I suppose he goes in for a good bit of adventure?

CHRISTOPHER ROBIN *(nodding).* The only thing he likes better than adventure is eating honey. *(Amends this, in response to the bear.) And* marmalade.

VOICE. Very well, then—I'll tell you a story about adventure *and* eating honey. *(His voice grows ominous.)* A story about how a frightening animal came to the forest—and about the terrible things that happened afterwards.

CHRISTOPHER ROBIN. Is it a scary story? Will I be able to sleep tonight?

VOICE. That depends. Let's get to the story. (*Pause.*) Once upon a time, a very long time ago—

CHRISTOPHER ROBIN. How long?

VOICE. About last Friday—

CHRISTOPHER ROBIN. Oh.

VOICE. —Winnie-the-Pooh lived in the forest under the name of Sanders.

CHRISTOPHER ROBIN. What does "under the name" mean?

VOICE (*after pause*). It means he had the name over the door in gold letters, and he lived under it.

CHRISTOPHER ROBIN (*nodding to indicate the bear*). He wasn't quite sure.

VOICE. One day he was out walking in the forest, when he came to an open place. And right on the edge of it, he saw a large oak tree. He stopped to listen...

CHRISTOPHER ROBIN. What was he listening to?

VOICE. A strange buzzing noise was coming from the top of the tree.

CHRISTOPHER ROBIN. A buzzing noise?

VOICE. Yes. If you'd stop interrupting, you'd be able to hear it. (*Sound of buzzing starts offstage, softly at first.*)

CHRISTOPHER ROBIN. I can! I wonder what it is?

VOICE. So did Winnie-the-Pooh...

(*CHRISTOPHER ROBIN exits R as the curtain rises, revealing a bare stage with a neutral background. DL, protruding from the wings, is part of the trunk of a tree. A branch with perhaps some leaves on it should show just before the tree disappears behind the proscenium. Attached well up on the tree is a sign with gold letters on it saying "Sanders." Underneath it is a child's rocking chair. DR is a similar tree, but without the sign. URC is another tree. Onstage, WINNIE-THE-POOH is DR, staring intently upward at something as lights come up full.)*

VOICE. He sat down, put his head between his paws, and began to think. *(POOH goes to hassock DR and sits down.)* He said to himself, "That buzzing noise means something. If there's a buzzing noise, somebody's making it—and the only reason for buzzing that I know of is because you're a bee—" *(POOH has adopted the "thinking position" as described above.)* Then he thought another long time and said, "The only reason for being a bee that I know of is to make honey—"

POOH *(rising and speaking for himself this time).* And the only reason for making honey is so *I* can eat it. *(At the thought of doing so, POOH rubs his paws together, licks his lips, and looks quite rapturous with anticipation. He makes a gurgling sound.)* Honey…*(Accompanies this with a couple of skipping steps in the direction of the tree DR.)* M-m-m…*(Stands still, struck by the thought.)* Funny, my liking it so much…*(He turns this into a song with a vague tune.)* Isn't it funny…*(Dances a step now and then, keeping time.)* How a bear likes honey…Buzz, buzz, buzz…I wonder why he does…*(He stops and frowns, beset by a problem. He goes over close to the tree and looks up.)* The question is: How do I get to the honey? *(Puts his chin on his hand and supports the elbow with the other hand.)* First, I'll have to climb the tree—*(Another upward look.)*— which will be a problem. And once I get to the *top* of the tree—*(He spots the hassock, places it under the tree and tries to reach the honey. When this doesn't work, he tumbles the hassock over toward URC.)*

(As if in answer to this, the buzzing gets quite loud for a moment—an angry tone about it. POOH is rather startled by this and backs away from the tree toward DC. As he is thinking it over, PIGLET enters from DL, looking rather excited.)

PIGLET *(calling to POOH)*. There you are, Pooh!

POOH *(preoccupied)*. Hello, Piglet.

PIGLET *(importantly, pausing DLC)*. I've got some news— *(Expecting a big reaction.)* A strange animal is coming to the forest.

POOH *(abstractedly, still looking at honey tree)*. Piglet, old friend...

PIGLET *(upset, moving to DC)*. I said, a *strange animal* is coming to the forest!

POOH. Hm-m-m-m—

PIGLET *(after a pause, going up close behind POOH and insisting)*. Aren't you going to ask *questions?*

POOH *(finally facing around to PIGLET)*. About what?

PIGLET *(rather wounded)*. You weren't listening.

POOH. Yes, I was. *(Points up at the tree.)* That's how I can tell it's up there.

PIGLET *(looking)*. What is?

POOH. Honey. *(Faces tree again.)*

PIGLET. *I* don't see honey. Just a lot of bees flying around—

POOH. Exactly.

PIGLET *(catching on)*. Oh.

POOH. There must be quite a lot of it—and freshly made— *(Working himself up to a frenzy of hungry anticipation, walking around in a circle.)*

PIGLET *(a gently admonishing tone)*. Pooh. You're forgetting.

POOH. —thick and golden...

PIGLET. Pooh...

POOH *(carried away)*. One delicious mouthful after another—

PIGLET *(tugging at his arm)*. Your diet!

POOH *(pausing beside PIGLET)*. What's that?

PIGLET. I thought you were going on a diet.

POOH. I am going on a diet. But not now. *(Resumes his hungry pacing, glancing up the tree occasionally.)*

PIGLET. Why not?

POOH *(lamely)*. Because—right *now* I'm hungry. *(More
firmly.)* That's not a good time to go on a diet.

PIGLET *(dubious)*. Oh. *(A true friend saying what POOH
would like to hear.)* I suppose tomorrow—after a good
night's rest?

POOH *(agreeing, with relief)*. And a good breakfast. *(Pauses
under the tree.)*

PIGLET. Yes. *(Crosses to DR and looks up at the tree.)* How
are you going to get up there?

POOH. Just what I've been wondering. If I could just reach
one of those branches—

PIGLET. If you were three feet taller—

POOH *(sadly)*. Which I'm not—

PIGLET *(bravely)*. Shall I give you a boost? *(POOH looks
hopeful.)* If you stood on my shoulders—*(He stops.)*

POOH. If I stood on your shoulders, I still couldn't reach it.
(Eyes the height for a moment.)

PIGLET. We'll think of something.

POOH. Thank you for offering, Piglet. You're a true friend.
*(PIGLET beams with pleasure. POOH pats his arm fondly,
tries to find a solution.)* Now, there *must* be—

(RABBIT bustles in DL, looking agitated.)

RABBIT *(muttering)*. I don't like it. I don't like the sound of it—

(RABBIT is followed by several FRIENDS and RELA-TIONS, who are dogging his steps.)

RABBIT *(hailing briskly from C)*. Pooh—Piglet!

POOH. Hello, Rabbit—*(When RABBIT stops, the FRIENDS and RELATIONS behind him bump into each other. He turns to them.)*

RABBIT. Now, run along and play. *(ALL clamor.)*

ANIMAL 1. But, Uncle Rabbit—

ANIMAL 2. What about the game?

Haley ANIMAL 1. You *promised*—

RABBIT. Later, later. There's an important matter I'll have to attend—

Brielle ANIMAL 1. But you *said*—

RABBIT *(shaking finger and raising his tone)*. I said—I'm busy. Run along and play! *(They know when he means business; they turn and leave DL, reluctantly.)* Now, then. *(Crosses to RC.)* I suppose you've heard?

POOH *(from DR)*. I'm not sure.

RABBIT. That a strange animal is coming to the forest—

PIGLET *(from DC)*. *I've* heard.

RABBIT *(disappointed)*. Oh, you have.

PIGLET *(pouring it out)*. That's what I was trying to tell you, Pooh. Her name is Kanga—*(Building this.)* She's one of the Fiercer Animals—

RABBIT. She's very tall—

PIGLET. *Enormous!*

POOH *(thinking this over very calmly, in a quiet tone)*. Any family?

RABBIT. I believe she has one offspring.

PIGLET. Is that all?

RABBIT. Its name is Roo. *(After pause.)* Imagine having a family of one! *(He is scornful of the idea.)*

POOH. How many in yours, Rabbit?

RABBIT. Hm-m-m...Sixteen.

PIGLET. Isn't it seventeen?

RABBIT. Perhaps. It's hard to keep *exact* count. *(Drops the subject.)* The important thing is, Kanga is coming—and she's...

POOH *(interrupting)*. I make it fifteen.

RABBIT. What?

POOH. Your family.

RABBIT *(impatiently)*. Never mind them!

POOH. I thought—

RABBIT *(cutting him off)*. The *important* thing is—Kanga is coming to live in the forest.

PIGLET. Yes!

POOH. And bringing an offspring named Roo—*(Looks up at the honey.)*

RABBIT. Yes—

POOH. And what's all the excitement about?

RABBIT. Because—Baby Roo isn't all she's bringing.

PIGLET. What else?

POOH *(hopefully)*. Groceries?

RABBIT *(hushed, fearful tone, after looking back over his shoulder)*. A bathtub.

PIGLET *(stuttering with fright)*. A b-bath—*bathtub?* What for?

RABBIT *(explaining, in a patronizing tone)*. Surely you know what a bathtub is for? You fill it with water—you get in—

PIGLET. I do *not!*

RABBIT *(rather enjoying PIGLET's nervous state)*. We hope not, Piglet. We *hope* not. *(Folds his arms and stares into space.)*

PIGLET *(crossing to POOH)*. You wouldn't let that happen to me, would you?

POOH *(firmly)*. You can count on me.

RABBIT. Now you see what the excitement is about. You see the necessity for taking action—

POOH. When is she supposed to arrive?

RABBIT *(hasn't any idea; pausing to think)*. Presently.

POOH. Does that mean she isn't here yet?

RABBIT. Of course.

POOH. What a relief. There was another little matter...*(A loud moan is heard offstage DL.)*

PIGLET. Help! *(Clings wildly to POOH. POOH and RABBIT stare in the direction of the sound.)*

VOICE *(offstage DL)*. Miserable. Miserable!

RABBIT. Someone's saying "miserable."

POOH. It must be Eeyore. He generally is.

(EEYORE enters DL, carrying a thistle and talking glumly to himself, but it sounds as if it were a continuation of POOH's speech.)

EEYORE. *Utterly* miserable. *(Stands apart, DL, waiting to be recognized.)*

POOH *(brightly)*. Good morning, Eeyore. *(Crosses to LC.)*

EEYORE *(raising his head, reluctantly)*. Good morning, Pooh Bear—*(Hangs head down again.)* if it is a good morning—*(Gives head a slight shake.)*—which I doubt.

RABBIT *(crossing to C)*. Surely it isn't that bad.

EEYORE. Perhaps not now. *(Flings his head up, with more emphasis.)* But it will be—when *she* gets here!

PIGLET *(hurrying to a place between POOH and RABBIT)*. He must mean Kanga.

EEYORE. Ah—you've heard.

RABBIT. About Kanga—yes.

POOH. And Baby Roo—

PIGLET *(the topper)*. *And* the bathtub!

EEYORE *(continuing)*. And the soap? *(EEYORE turns his back while OTHERS digest this new bombshell. He talks in the other direction.)* I found out by chance.

POOH. Soap?

EEYORE. No one would bother to tell *me*.

PIGLET *(in a faint, squealing voice)*. *Soap?*

EEYORE *(turning)*. You didn't know about it?

RABBIT. *What* soap?

EEYORE. You didn't know she carries a cake of the stuff in her pocket? *(To himself again.)* Well, none of us knows *every*thing. *(Munches on the thistle he has been carrying.)*

RABBIT *(to OTHERS)*. This is terrible!

PIGLET. Awful!

RABBIT. It couldn't be worse!

EEYORE. It could be *much* worse. And probably will be. *(He chews dolefully.)*

RABBIT *(annoyed)*. Eeyore, *must* you eat thistles?

EEYORE. All donkeys eat them. And I happen to be *especially* fond of them.

RABBIT. No wonder you're so gloomy. *(EEYORE stares steadily at him.)* How anyone can help seeing the dark side of things, if they eat thistles all the time…*(EEYORE, very wounded, lies down on his stomach, burying his head in his arms.)*

EEYORE *(sobbingly)*. That's right. Deprive me of the only pleasure I have left. Why not give up *everything?* *(He is so broken that RABBIT gives a sigh of "What can you do?")*

POOH *(crossing to DL where EEYORE is lying)*. He didn't mean it.

RABBIT (*crossing to just upstage of EEYORE*). I didn't mean it! I apologize! (*Tries harder, as EEYORE just sniffs disconsolately.*) Eat thistles—please! (*EEYORE sits up and takes out another thistle, and after wiping his eyes on his arm, begins to munch.*)

EEYORE (*after a pause*). Very well. It's terrible kind of you. (*Takes another bite. RABBIT wipes his forehead with relief.*)

RABBIT (*moving back to C*). Now. Where were we? (*PIGLET has been too nervous to bother about EEYORE's persecution-mania and has moved to C.*)

PIGLET (*shakily*). Soap...

RABBIT. Yes. I'm afraid the time has come—(*He lets this statement hang ominously and looks over to POOH, who is still standing by EEYORE, watching his chewing with fascination. POOH turns.*)

POOH (*suddenly*). What time is it, by the way?

RABBIT. Eleven o'clock.

POOH. Just as I thought. I generally have a little something around eleven...(*Crosses to DRC and looks up at the honey.*)

RABBIT. When I say "The time has come," I don't mean eleven o'clock. I mean that danger is threatening!

POOH. Danger?

PIGLET. The bathtub...the soap...

RABBIT. Yes!

POOH (*thoughtfully*). That sort of thing is unpleasant. But dangerous?

(*OWL's sonorous, booming voice is heard from just onstage UR where he has entered slowly during the last few speeches.*)

OWL. What about the bottle of poison?

RABBIT *(not noticing who has said this, arguing with POOH)*. Yes! What about the—*(He stops.)*

PIGLET *(looking around)*. Who said that?

OWL *(coming further onstage to RC)*. Who, indeed?

RABBIT and POOH. Owl!

EEYORE. I wish he *wouldn't*...this barging in suddenly—

OWL *(coming downstage)*. I didn't barge in. I've been here for some time.

EEYORE. Then why not speak up sooner?

OWL *(frowning at EEYORE)*. There was nothing whatever to say.

PIGLET. But you said "bottle of poison"!

OWL *(nodding slowly)*. I did. Because she has one. A small bottle—filled with brown stuff.

POOH. How do you know it's—

OWL *(talking over this)*. *Clearly* written on the label is the word "Poison."

RABBIT. I can't believe it! *(RABBIT, POOH, PIGLET and EEYORE form a compact group DLC.)*

PIGLET. It must be true—he knows how to read—

POOH. And write—

RABBIT. And spell—

EEYORE *(scoffing)*. Spell his name, perhaps...W-O-L...that's not so hard. He goes to pieces over words like "measles" or "buttered toast"...*(As they ALL regard OWL doubtfully, he draws himself up and continues.)*

OWL. In addition to the word "Poison" on the label, there was a picture.

POOH. What sort of picture?

OWL. The bones of some dead creature.

RABBIT. Bones!

POOH. Who would want that sort of picture?

RABBIT. Who would want a bathtub!

EEYORE. Or soap...

OWL. Or a bottle of poison.

PIGLET. Kanga! She must be a terrible Monster—

OWL. The evidence clearly indicates that she is Up To No Good. *(NOTE: When "talking in capitals," one talks slowly, importantly, and with great emphasis, enunciating each word with clarity and dignity and allowing a slight pause between each word.)*

PIGLET. What shall we do?

RABBIT *(hopping up and down)*. Do? We must organize. Deal with the matter—

EEYORE. The worst is yet to come.

RABBIT *(ignoring him)*. Take action—we—must—

OWL *(advancing a step or two toward them)*. Stop! Listen to me. We shall follow the Customary Procedure. *(The OTHERS look mystified, but are quiet.)* In other words—*(They look at him now, hopeful they can understand the "other words.")*—we'll Have a Meeting.

RABBIT. A Meeting?

OWL. One can't take Action without first having a Meeting.

RABBIT *(interrupting with a protest and taking a step toward OWL)*. I still think—

OWL *(cutting him off severely)*. As you all know! *(RABBIT is properly squelched and scuttles back to the safety of the crowd.)* We'll begin now. *(He raises a wing majestically.)* The Meeting will come to order! *(RABBIT sits down beside EEYORE, who has been sitting throughout.)*

POOH *(anxious whisper to PIGLET)*. How?

PIGLET *(responding in a whisper)*. I think we sit down. *(Points to EEYORE and RABBIT.)*

POOH. Oh. *(He and PIGLET sit down. POOH sits in a spot toward DC.)*

OWL *(in his element).* Now, then…*(Looks down at the ground.)* Let me see…Ahem…*(The looks of disgust on everybody's faces increase, and RABBIT stirs restlessly. EEYORE makes a loud smacking sound over a thistle, and POOH looks longingly at him as the lights dim. OWL drones on and on, and the buzzing of the bees increases until it nearly drowns him out. POOH turns his gaze from OWL toward the top of the tree as if pulled by a magnet.)* Whereas…Hmm—I daresay we should start with the first order of business, which is…*(His voice fades to an indistinct mumble. POOH rises and walks off toward the tree DR, exiting as if he were in a trance. After his exit, the buzzing gradually dies down. OWL is still talking, and the other three ANIMALS have gone from sitting positions to being sprawled on the ground. EEYORE stifles a yawn. The lights brighten and OWL speaks audibly again.)* And, as I was saying—

RABBIT. What *were* you saying?

(ANIMAL 3 and 4 stick their heads onstage DL and listen.)

EEYORE. That's what I'd like to know.

RABBIT *(getting up resolutely).* If you ask *me*—

OWL *(crushing him again).* If we ask you—what will happen? *(RABBIT continues to hop up and down.)* Excitement. A good deal of hopping up and down. *(RABBIT stops.)* Commotion. *(OWL shakes his head, satisfied.)* The important thing is to remain calm—*(A faint cracking sound is heard offstage DR. ANIMALS 3 and ANIMAL 4, still peeking out from DL, look up sharply. The noise comes from high up.)*—to keep our heads. *(Another cracking sound. One ANIMAL points up at it.)*

PIGLET *(nervously, getting up)*. What was that? *(EEYORE rises also.)*

RABBIT. I heard something!

OWL. Above all, to follow Customary Procedure—

POOH *(a faint cry from high up, offstage DR)*. Oh, help!

RABBIT. Help?

PIGLET. Help! She's coming—Kanga's coming! *(Begins to shake all over.)*

OWL. She can't come now. We haven't finished the Meeting.

RABBIT *(quickly)*. I suggest we finish it somewhere else!

OWL *(very quickly)*. A very good suggestion. *(RABBIT, OWL and EEYORE start off, trying to move with calmness and dignity, but looking nervously behind them. ANIMALS 3 and 4 have disappeared off L.)*

EEYORE. Aren't you coming, Piglet?

PIGLET *(from DLC)*. I can't—c-can't move—*(The cracking sound gets very loud, and turns into a loud crash. ALL abandon their pretense of calm, and run out DL with a leap except for PIGLET, who throws himself flat on his face and covers his head with his arms.)*

(After a pause, POOH enters. He is limping slightly, brushing himself off, and looking annoyed.)

POOH *(as he wanders to R)*. Bother!

PIGLET *(uncovering one eye, and peeking out)*. Is that you?

POOH. Yes. At least, most of me seems to be here.

PIGLET *(uncovering the other eye)*. Wh-what happened?

POOH. A slight accident. *(As PIGLET struggles up.)* You noticed the small tree, growing very close to the large one— the one with the honey at the top—

PIGLET. What small tree?

POOH. It fell over.

PIGLET. That dreadful noise—was a small tree falling over?

POOH. I was *in* the small tree.

PIGLET *(an exclamation of relief)*. Oh!

POOH. I thought if I could get to the top, I might just reach over and—*(In illustrating this, POOH stands on one foot, with one paw outstretched. He looks at this paw; an idea occurs.)* I wonder...*(He raises his paw higher, as if holding something.)* It might...*(Raises the paw even higher, as if something were pulling him up in the air.)* Could it?

PIGLET. Could it what?

POOH *(coming DC)*. There's only one way to find out. Piglet, do you have such a thing as a balloon about you?

PIGLET. A *balloon? (Shakes head, mystified.)* No.

POOH. Christopher Robin! If I know anything at all, Christopher Robin will have a balloon! *(Starts DL.)*

PIGLET. Wait. Where are you going?

POOH. To borrow it.

PIGLET. Don't leave me here alone. I mean, I'm coming with you!

POOH. That's very kind of you, Piglet. *(As PIGLET joins him, he turns suddenly.)* By the way, what happened to the others?

PIGLET. Others?

POOH. Owl and Rabbit and Eeyore. Is the Meeting all over?

PIGLET. They decided to continue the meeting somewhere else.

POOH. Oh. Perhaps you'd rather join them—

PIGLET. No! I'd rather stay with you. *(Amending.)* To keep you company.

POOH. Splendid!

PIGLET. And would it be too much—if I held onto your hand—

POOH. Not at all. *(He starts out DL with PIGLET clinging to his hand and looking back nervously. POOH is in good*

spirits, and starts to sing again as he trots off.) "Isn't it
funny—how a bear likes honey—" *(His voice fades off.)*

(ANIMALS 1 and 2 enter DL.)

ANIMAL 1 *(looking back over his shoulder and pouting in-
dignantly)*. It's not fair. Uncle Rabbit said he was too busy
to play a game with us—

ANIMAL 2. But he can't be very busy! *(Pauses UC.)*

(ANIMAL 3 enters with ANIMAL 4 beside him.)

ANIMAL 3. A lot you know about it.

ANIMAL 1. We just saw him running a race with Eeyore and
Owl.

ANIMAL 4 *(LC, in a superior tone)*. That wasn't a race.

ANIMAL 2. You should have seen them! I never saw Uncle
Rabbit run so fast! *(Demonstrates by running to UR and
back to RC.)*

ANIMAL 1. And Eeyore…I never saw him run at *all*.

ANIMAL 3 *(UC)*. Ha! They thought the Kanga was chasing
them.

ANIMAL 1. Kanga?

ANIMAL 2. What's that?

ANIMAL 4. Never mind. I'll bet there's no such thing.

ANIMAL 3. Me, too!

ANIMAL 4. All that about soap—and bathtubs—and poison—

ANIMAL 3. Whoever heard of stuff like that! *(ANIMALS 1
and 2 look rather anxious.)*

ANIMAL 1. Did you?

ANIMAL 2. No—

(As they finish speaking, RABBIT enters hurriedly from DL and crosses toward DR.)

RABBIT *(as he crosses)*. We went the wrong way. *(He keeps glancing fearfully behind him as he goes out DR.)*

ANIMAL 4 *(gesturing after RABBIT)*. What's the matter with him?

ANIMAL 3. He's just a fraidy cat.

(OWL enters DL and hastens along to DR.)

OWL. Hurry! It's coming—it's coming! *(He hastens out DR.)*

(PRODUCTION NOTE: If extra characters are available and it is desired to use them, the above scene may be staged by having one or more animals take the places of RABBIT, OWL, and EEYORE. RABBIT's line "We went the wrong way" should be replaced by "Better hurry, it's coming!" The earlier exit of RABBIT, OWL, and EEYORE should be made DR if the extra characters are used.)

(The FOUR onstage look at each other. Then ANIMAL 2 (the skunk) holds up his paw as he sniffs the air.

ANIMAL 2. Something *is* coming—

ANIMAL 1. What?

ANIMAL 2. Something *strange*—

ANIMAL 3 *(skeptically)*. How do *you* know?

ANIMAL 2. I'm very sensitive to unpleasant smells. And I've never come across anything like *this* before—

ANIMAL 1. Is it a Kanga?

ANIMAL 3. Oh, sure! When there isn't any such thing?

(EEYORE enters from DL and crosses to exit DR.)

EEYORE *(crossing)*. Oh, I'll never make it. I'll be caught and then—Oh, dear!

(OPTIONAL: Another assortment of ANIMALS runs across the stage.)

ANIMAL 4 *(to ANIMAL 3)*. Maybe Uncle Rabbit wasn't fooling.

ANIMAL 3. Sure he was—he made the whole thing up.

ANIMAL 1. He wouldn't do that.

ANIMAL 4 *(to ANIMAL 3)*. He doesn't know everything...

ANIMAL 3 *(bristling)*. He knows more than you do!

ANIMAL 4. And more than you do—and that's not much—

ANIMAL 3. You take that back!

ANIMAL 4. Make me! *(They begin to fight—wrestling about, making grunting noises, etc., as they roll on the ground LC.)*

ANIMAL 1 *(crossing to URC)*. Shouldn't we stop them?

ANIMAL 2. Remember what Christopher Robin says—*(Also moves to URC.)* "Never interfere in other animals' business." *(Another ANIMAL may go by, at this point, from DL to DR, waving its arms and shouting, "It's coming! It's coming!")*

ANIMAL 1 *(to ANIMAL 2)*. I just happened to remember an old badger hole about four miles from here—Look, a flock of birds! *(Points overhead DL and moves his pointing finger across to DR, as if the flock of birds were rapidly flying from DL to DR.)*

ANIMAL 2 *(as they follow the flight with their eyes)*. Is it a large hole?

ANIMAL 1. Large enough for both of us, anyway. *(They join hands and run off DR. It seems that the exodus is over, as*

*there is general quiet. ANIMALS 3 and 4 are still scuffling
quietly. At last ANIMAL 3 is on top of ANIMAL 4.)*
ANIMAL 3. Give up?
ANIMAL 4 *(panting).* All right—

*(ANIMALS 3 and 4 are intent on each other, and don't
notice when KANGA enters DL. She is carrying a round tin
washtub in her right hand and pulling BABY ROO along
with her left hand. She stops DL, looks at the wrestling
ANIMALS and frowns.)*

ANIMAL 4. What were we fighting about?
ANIMAL 3. I forget.
ANIMAL 4. Something about a—a—*(Sees KANGA.)*
ANIMAL 3. Only there wasn't any such thing—*(Also sees
KANGA.)*—any such—*(ANIMAL 4 leaps up and scampers
off DR, ANIMAL 3 does the same.)*
KANGA *(with matronly disgust).* Well! *(Walks to C.)* Dis-
graceful. Perfectly disgraceful.
ROO *(eagerly).* Mama, can I go play with them? *(Starts after
them, pulling across KANGA till her hold on his hand
stops him.)*
KANGA *(pulling him back to her left side).* Certainly not, Roo.
ROO. But you said when we came to the forest, I'd have
someone to play with. *(Points after ANIMALS 3 and 4.)*
And I haven't *seen* anybody but them. Maybe nobody else
lives here!
KANGA. Nonsense. There are plenty of animals in the forest.
ROO. Then where are they? *(Holds out his hands, looking
around.)*
KANGA *(frowning, puzzled tone).* I simply can't understand
it. *(To ROO.)* But never mind—you wouldn't want to play
with those filthy creatures—

ROO. Well—

KANGA (*shaking her head with disgust*). They look as if they never had a bath in their lives—

ROO (*muttering to himself*). Darn it! (*KANGA, startled, puts down the washtub near the hassock with a clang.*)

KANGA (*bending down, looking at ROO ominously*). What did you say?

ROO (*hanging his head*). Nothing.

KANGA. I heard it, Roo. (*She drags him to where the hassock is, sits on it and reaches into the washtub. ROO still hangs his head.*) And you know what that means. (*She pulls out a soapy washrag [a clean washrag with whipped cream from a pressure can].*) When our mouth says ugly things, we must wash it. Mustn't we, Roo? (*All of this is said in a calm, pleasant but very maternal tone.*) There we are—(*Washing out his mouth. ROO squirms, but she has a good grip on him. ROO makes a horrible face. KANGA notices something on his knee and points to it.*) My goodness, what did you do to your knee? (*ROO burbles something through his mouthful of soap.*) A nasty scratch, dear. (*She reaches into her pocket and pulls out a bottle of iodine. At the sight of it, ROO begins to burble frantically.*) We'll have to put something on it.

ROO (*as KANGA opens the bottle*). Wow-w-w—

KANGA. We don't want it to get infected, do we?

ROO. Not *iodine!* Not—

KANGA (*dabbing the knee with iodine*). Just a touch—

ROO. Ouch!

KANGA. There's a brave little Roo. (*Puts the bottle away as ROO struggles about, hopping up and down.*) Think how lucky you are. You wouldn't want to be like *those* poor creatures—with no one to look after you properly. Aren't you thankful? *(ROO mumbles something. KANGA reacts, sharply again.)* What was that?

ROO. Thankful.

KANGA. If only something could be done for them. If I could just get hold of them for one day—

ROO. Would they have a bath?

KANGA. Plenty of soap and good hot water—

ROO *(wiping his face carefully).* Then could I play with them?

KANGA *(hesitating).* After a dusting of disinfectant powder.

ROO. Would they have oatmeal for breakfast?

KANGA. And a big spoonful of Strengthening Medicine-*(Carried away.)* Oh, the things I could do for them!

ROO. Would they be thankful, too?

KANGA *(a momentary hesitation).* Perhaps not at first. Not right away, but...*(Pulls herself back to reality.)*...no use thinking about it. I couldn't take care of all the animals in the forest, wherever they are...

ROO. How about just one?

KANGA *(looking around the stage).* Dear little Roo—we'll see.

ROO *(wistfully).* One that's my own size. It would be so nice—

KANGA. Maybe we can arrange for you to have a playmate—*(She stops and looks at tree C.)* I think this will do nicely.

ROO. What will?

KANGA. For our new home.

ROO. Are we going to live here?

KANGA. Let's see...It has shade—privacy—plenty of water in that stream...*(As she goes up to the tree, ROO wanders off toward UL and picks up something.)*

ROO *(delighted, squealing).* Here's a caterpillar!

KANGA *(turning suddenly).* Goodness, don't touch! *(ROO puts it down quickly, with a look of dismay.)* If you touch it, you'll need a bath. *(ROO hides his hands behind his back.)* And there's so much to do, what with sweeping this place out—*(As KANGA goes back to the tree, ROO watches the caterpillar crawl away, taking the direction of all the other refugees. ROO walks slowly behind it, watching it with mournful eyes.)*—getting settled—

ROO *(hearing something).* Mama—*(A faint sound in the distance DL: POOH's voice, singing, "Isn't it funny— How a bear likes honey— ")*

KANGA. Don't bother me now, dear.

ROO. Somebody's coming!

KANGA. Really?

ROO. I hear them—and that means somebody lives in the forest! *(KANGA listens, hears something, too.)*

KANGA. Then stay near me, Roo.

ROO. Why? *(KANGA rolls her eyes to heaven, and lifts her hands with a typical parental gesture.)*

KANGA. One must be patient, and explain everything... *(Looks at ROO, a "patient" tone.)* Because if they see you, they'll know we live here. And if they know we live here, I shall have to invite them to tea. *And* I don't want to have company yet, because everything is a mess. *And—(Goes off DL, or off UC if practical.)*

ROO *(he can't bear it).* All right, I'm *coming.* I just *asked.* *(Follows KANGA off.)*

(POOH enters DL, singing jovially, with PIGLET and CHRISTOPHER ROBIN, who carries a large blue balloon and a popgun. NOTE: If filled with air, the balloon should be held as if it were helium-filled and quite buoyant.)

POOH *(singing).* "Buzz, buzz, buzz—I wonder why he does—"

PIGLET. Ssh!

POOH *(starting the song over, with great vigor)*. "Isn't it funny—how a bear likes honey—" *(They pause RC and face about toward the honey tree DR.)*

PIGLET *(tugging at POOH)*. Please! I wish you wouldn't sing so loudly.

POOH *(near tree DR)*. "Buzz, buzz, buzz—" *(Shrugs, then accedes to PIGLET's request.)* Rum-tum-tiddle-um-tum. *(This is a sort of finisher to the song, uttered quietly.)*

CHRISTOPHER ROBIN *(fondly, near POOH)*. Silly old bear!

POOH. Are you still feeling jumpy, Piglet?

PIGLET *(from C)*. I hate to be cowardly, but I couldn't help noticing—As we were coming this way, everybody else was going *that* way...*(Points in the direction of the general exodus.)*

POOH. I noticed, myself.

CHRISTOPHER ROBIN. They were, were they?

POOH. It's all this talk about Kanga.

CHRISTOPHER ROBIN. Where did you hear about Kanga?

(KANGA peeks out at the mention of her name.)

POOH. You know how it is—stories get about in the forest— you can't believe everything you hear—*(Takes a few waltz-ing steps toward his tree DR.)*

PIGLET *(confidential)*. Christopher Robin—

CHRISTOPHER ROBIN. Yes?

PIGLET. Is there a Kanga coming to the forest?

CHRISTOPHER ROBIN. You'll have to find out for yourself, Piglet.

PIGLET. You mean—

POOH. If Christopher Robin knows a secret, you don't expect him to tell, do you?

PIGLET *(thinking a moment, rushing wildly to POOH)*. Let's get out of here. Let's go that way! *(Waves frantically DR.)*

POOH. As soon as I reach that honey. After all, if we're going on a journey I've got to have a little something to sustain me.

PIGLET *(with pathetic despair)*. If I weren't such a coward, I'd go alone!

POOH. Stop worrying, Piglet. You're safe as long as you're with me. *(Cajoling tone.)* Don't I always keep you out of trouble?

PIGLET. What about that time we—

POOH *(interrupting)*. Don't I *usually* keep you out of trouble?

PIGLET. Well—

POOH. You can depend on me.

PIGLET. You're sure?

POOH. Quite sure. *(Crosses to RC near CHRISTOPHER ROBIN and looks at the balloon speculatively.)* Now let me see—

CHRISTOPHER ROBIN. Do you really think it will work?

POOH. I think—when you go after honey, it's very important not to let the bees know you're coming. If you have a blue balloon, they might think you're only part of the sky and not notice!

CHRISTOPHER ROBIN. Wouldn't they notice *you* underneath the balloon?

POOH. You never can tell, with bees…*(Thinks a moment, then lies down on the ground, rolling about.)*

CHRISTOPHER ROBIN. What are you doing?

POOH *(rubbing dirt all over his arms and face)*. I'll try to look like a small black cloud.

(KANGA, who has come a step onstage to see all this, makes a terrible face of disapproval and steps back again.)

POOH. *That* will deceive them.

CHRISTOPHER ROBIN *(as POOH reaches for the balloon).* Well, good luck...*(POOH takes balloon and is immediately pulled. He takes a few running steps and a leap. PIGLET ducks around to C to keep out from under.)*

POOH *(as he leaps).* Here—I—go! *(He is pulled up and off-stage DR. [A ladder from which he can give his next few lines will help the illusion of height.] CHRISTOPHER ROBIN and PIGLET watch him float upward, their heads tilting back as they follow the ascent.)*

CHRISTOPHER ROBIN *(grinning at the sight).* Hooray!

POOH'S VOICE *(calling from offstage DR).* Isn't this fine? What do I look like?

CHRISTOPHER ROBIN. You look like a bear holding onto a balloon.

POOH'S VOICE *(after a pause, worried).* Not—like a small black cloud in a blue sky?

CHRISTOPHER ROBIN. Not very much.

PIGLET. I wish he'd hurry up.

POOH'S VOICE. Perhaps from up here it looks different...

CHRISTOPHER ROBIN. Can't you get any closer to the tree? You're at least ten feet away from it—and a bit too high.

POOH'S VOICE. I'm trying...

CHRISTOPHER ROBIN. Maybe a breeze will come along, and blow you a bit closer...

POOH'S VOICE. When?

CHRISTOPHER ROBIN. You'll just have to wait.

PIGLET *(with anxiety).* We can't wait long—

(As PIGLET and CHRISTOPHER ROBIN watch POOH, ROO comes in and approaches PIGLET, looking fascinated.)

ROO (*tugging at PIGLET's arm*). What's your name?

PIGLET (*not registering, but answering automatically*). Piglet.

ROO (*calling to KANGA excitedly*). Mama—I've found a playmate!

CHRISTOPHER ROBIN (*turning and patting him fondly*). Hallo there, Roo—(*Crosses back to DR to watch POOH.*)

PIGLET. Roo…(*He turns.*) Roo?

(*KANGA comes in quickly.*)

KANGA (*with an approving smile*). Isn't that nice? He's just the right size.

PIGLET (*with growing horror*). Roo!

ROO. That's my name.

PIGLET. But if you're Roo—she must be—(*Looks at KANGA, who is moving toward him purposefully, and takes one step backwards before he stops and begins to tremble.*)

KANGA (*to CHRISTOPHER ROBIN, in a tone of reprimand*). You haven't introduced us properly.

CHRISTOPHER ROBIN. Kanga—

PIGLET. *Kanga!*

CHRISTOPHER ROBIN (*continuing*). —and Roo, this is Piglet. (*Points at POOH.*) And Pooh.

POOH'S VOICE. Did you call me?

PIGLET (*calling*). Pooh, I think you'd better come down!

KANGA. I hadn't intended to have company just yet, but Roo seems so anxious—

ROO. Give him a bath right now, Mama, so I can play with him!

KANGA. Very well. (*She gets a good grip on PIGLET. To ROO.*) Run and get some water. (*ROO hurries off DL.*)

PIGLET. A bath? Me—a bath—

KANGA. The tub is all ready. What are you squirming for?

CHRISTOPHER ROBIN. He—ah—never had a bath before.

KANGA. Well! Then it's about time!

CHRISTOPHER ROBIN. It may be a shock. That is, he won't like it...

KANGA. How do you know—when he's never had one?

CHRISTOPHER ROBIN. I suppose you're right...

PIGLET *(as KANGA starts calmly to drag him to washtub URC)*. Pooh! You've got to come down—right now!

POOH'S VOICE. I know, Piglet—but how can I get down?

PIGLET. Help! Let go of the balloon!

POOH'S VOICE. If I let go, I won't be of much help to any-one...

PIGLET *(holding KANGA to a standstill by exerting all his force)*. Christopher Robin—please! *Shoot* the balloon—

POOH'S VOICE. Yes—if you can shoot the balloon, I might float down gradually—

KANGA *(referring to her struggle with PIGLET)*. Honestly, such a time...

CHRISTOPHER ROBIN. I'm not supposed to interfere— *(Takes a sympathetic look at the struggling PIGLET.)* But I'll try—*(Takes aim and fires the popgun.)*

POOH'S VOICE. *Ow!*

CHRISTOPHER ROBIN. Did I miss?

POOH'S VOICE. You didn't exactly miss, but you missed the *balloon*—

PIGLET. Try it again.

CHRISTOPHER ROBIN. I'm out of ammunition.

PIGLET. Oh-h-h!

KANGA. I've never seen *anything* like it—

PIGLET *(as he is dragged farther and farther URC)*. Pooh, you've got to come down! You said you'd protect me— you said you'd keep me out of trouble—

POOH'S VOICE. But I *can't!* I can't get *down! (As PIGLET is forced into the bathtub.)* Oh, dear!

(ROO comes rushing on with a pitcher of water and hands it to KANGA.)

PIGLET You *promised*—you—*(As the water is poured over him, he wails mournfully.)*

CHRISTOPHER ROBIN. I'll go and get more ammunition.

POOH'S VOICE. Hurry!

CHRISTOPHER ROBIN. I'll *try*—*(He hurries out DR, with one last worried look in the direction of PIGLET.)*

KANGA. Now stop wiggling. Or you'll get soap in your eyes. This is just the beginning—first the bath—then the diet— the Strengthening Medicine—This is the beginning, that's all—*(The curtain starts down/or lights start down.)*

PIGLET. Wowww—blub-blub—Pooh, this is *your* fault—all your—*Pooh! Help! Help! (His protests turn into a gurgling sound.)*

CURTAIN if intermission is desired—
otherwise lights dim to black—

ACT TWO

SCENE: *Spot on CHRISTOPHER ROBIN, again sitting on hassock DR, the same place he was at the start of Act One. He is holding his teddy bear—and looking sad and worried.*

VOICE *(narrator, offstage).* —And while you went home to look for more ammunition, Pooh stayed up in the air holding onto his balloon...

CHRISTOPHER ROBIN. And what about poor Piglet—

VOICE *(sober, sympathetic).* Yes, poor Piglet...*(A sigh.)* He'd never been clean before.

CHRISTOPHER ROBIN. Did it take me very long to get more ammunition?

VOICE. Quite a while. By the time you got back—and shot the balloon—

CHRISTOPHER ROBIN. I didn't miss the next time?

VOICE. No.

CHRISTOPHER ROBIN. I'm glad of that.

VOICE. Pooh floated down to the ground—but he'd been holding onto that balloon for such a long time that his arms stayed up in the air.

CHRISTOPHER ROBIN. Like this? *(Holds the teddy bear's paws up over its head.)*

VOICE. Like that.

CHRISTOPHER ROBIN. Wasn't he uncomfortable?

VOICE. Very uncomfortable. But after all, it was his own fault. There was his best friend, in grave difficulty—and

33

where was Pooh? Up in the air. All because he wanted to eat honey. You'll have to admit it served him right.

CHRISTOPHER ROBIN (*wagging a reproachful finger at the teddy bear*). I'm afraid it *did* serve you right!

(*If there is no intermission, leave curtain open and bring up lights as CHRISTOPHER ROBIN exits R. The scene is a different part of the forest, so the sign "Sanders" has been taken down from the tree. The tree that was URC has been moved to LC and a gnarled aerial root which forms a medium-sized hole has been attached to the C side of this tree. Over it is a sign saying "Rabbit Hole." A small rocking chair should be placed UC, and against the back wall URC is a small cupboard. As in Act One, there are trees DR and DL framing the stage. OWL is standing unobtrusively at UR corner of the stage. POOH enters from DL, his arms held up in the air as though still clinging to the balloon.*)

POOH. It serves me right! (*Continues to reproach himself.*) Pooh Bear—how could you do a thing like that?

OWL (*echoes POOH from his place at rear of stage*). How *could* you?

POOH (*answering, thinking it's himself*). I don't know.

OWL (*coming a few steps toward DRC*). Of course, you were hungry...

POOH (*from DLC*). Yes, I was hungry...

OWL. But being hungry is no excuse for Deserting Your Best Friend.

POOH (*in an agony of self-reproach*). Not even if you're *terribly* hungry?

OWL. No excuse.

POOH. Practically *starving!*

OWL. At any rate, it's a very bad excuse.

(EEYORE peeks out from DR.)

EEYORE. A hard fall, was it?

POOH. What's that, Eeyore?

EEYORE *(coming on stage to DR)*. One often talks to oneself after a bad fall. Landed on your head, perhaps?

POOH. I landed in a sitting position.

EEYORE *(walking around him slowly)*. Any severe pain?

POOH. No.

EEYORE *(shaking his head pessimistically)*. I was afraid of that. The worst sort of injuries—no severe pain—no pain at *all...*

POOH. The only trouble with me is, I can't get my paws back to where they belong. And I *must* get them down. Something has to be done about Piglet—right away!

OWL. Piglet.

EEYORE. Poor little Piglet.

POOH. You see, Kanga captured him—*quite by accident*— He's in a terrible predicament. *(He crosses to RC.)*

EEYORE. In hot water?

POOH. How did you know?

EEYORE. A-ha.

POOH. He must be rescued, right away.

OWL *(nodding)*. Immediately.

EEYORE *(also nodding)*. Without wasting a minute.

POOH. The only question is, how shall we rescue him? *(EEYORE backs up till he is DR.)*

EEYORE. We?

OWL *(still RC)*. How shall *you* rescue him?

EEYORE. Yes, *that's* the question.

OWL *(advancing a step toward POOH)*. Since Piglet is your best friend, we know *you* want to be the one.

POOH. Oh. *(He thinks this over with a good bit of surprise. His arms drop, at last.)*

EEYORE *(also advancing a step toward POOH)*. Especially since the whole thing was your fault. *(A distant squeal from PIGLET, offstage L.)*

PIGLET'S VOICE. No! No-no-no-o-o-o! *(Suddenly cut off. POOH, EEYORE and OWL look in the direction of the noise.)*

OWL. You'd better hurry.

EEYORE. If it isn't too late...which it probably is.

POOH. But how? What shall I do?

EEYORE. *Much* too late.

OWL. Why not go to Kanga—explain the situation—

POOH. How?

OWL. Just say, "Kanga, you have something that doesn't belong to you. That isn't *your* Piglet—that's *our* Piglet—" And then—

POOH *(warily)*. Then what?

OWL. She'll have to let Piglet go. At least, she *ought* to.

POOH. There's a difference between *"ought* to" and *"have* to."

EEYORE. And Kangas are generally regarded as one of the Fiercer Animals.

OWL. Quite true.

POOH. I wouldn't want to do anything foolish.

OWL. You've already done something foolish. And I just happened to remember—

POOH. What?

OWL. Bears are *also* regarded as one of the Fiercer Animals.

POOH. Bears?

OWL. *Very* fierce.

POOH. Me?

OWL. They snarl—growl—do all sorts of nasty things. Can't *you* growl, Pooh?

POOH. I don't know.

OWL. Try.

POOH (*a cozy sort of growl, or even a purr*). Gr-r-r. (*EEYORE and OWL frown.*) How was that?

EEYORE. It wasn't much.

POOH (*improving it slightly*). Gr-r-r.

OWL. Let's have just a little snarl.

POOH (*baring his teeth this time*). Gr-r-r-r-r!

OWL (*to EEYORE*). Better, don't you think?

EEYORE. A growl ought to be bloodcurdling.

POOH (*really putting some stuff in it*). Gr-r-r—

OWL (*signaling that this is it*). Ah!

POOH (*carried away*). Gr-r-R-R-R!!! (*As EEYORE and OWL recoil, POOH shakes himself and looks around, quite startled.*)

OWL. What's the matter?

POOH (*slightly injured tone*). I frightened myself.

OWL. That's a good sign.

POOH. The question is, will I frighten Kanga?

OWL. Certainly. There's no doubt in my mind.

EEYORE. And a good thing, too. (*Looking off DL, gesturing.*) Here she comes!

POOH. Who?

OWL. Where?

EEYORE. Kanga. She's coming this way.

OWL. Come, Eeyore—

POOH (*as EEYORE starts off DR with OWL*). You aren't going?

EEYORE. We'll be around if you need us.

POOH. Around where?

OWL (*hastening off DR with EEYORE*). Somewhere...
    (*POOH starts after them, but at the edge of the stage he
    hesitates, turns around and braces himself. He practices a
    snarl, which reassures him, and stands firmly ready to con-
    front KANGA.*)

    (*KANGA enters DLC with ROO and PIGLET each holding
    one of her hands. PIGLET is practically unrecognizable. If
    possible, he has on snowy white coveralls, and there is a
    huge bow tied around his neck.*)

KANGA (*still holding their hands*). Now then, chins up—
    chests out—make the most of every step.
ROO (*puffing*). I can't go any faster—
KANGA. Nonsense.
PIGLET (*calling out at the sight of POOH*). Pooh—it's *Pooh!*
    (*Lunges forward in POOH's direction, but KANGA re-
    trieves him with a firm grasp.*)
KANGA. Why, so it is.
PIGLET. At last—(*POOH crosses to C and, folding his arms
    over his chest, assumes a wide stance, facing KANGA.*)
KANGA. Would you mind? You're blocking the path.
POOH. Er—um—
KANGA. After all, it doesn't belong to you—does it?
POOH (*unfolding his arms so he can gesture freely*). That's
    what I wanted to explain. You have something that doesn't
    belong to you—I mean—
KANGA. Whatever *is* he talking about!
POOH. Piglet.
PIGLET. Poo-oo-oh!
POOH. You are Piglet?
PIGLET. Of course I am!

POOH. I just wanted to be sure. You don't *look* like Piglet. *(PIGLET tries to pull loose from KANGA.)*

KANGA. Now, now—mustn't let go of my hand.

POOH. But you ought to let him go. He isn't your Piglet. He's *our* Piglet—

KANGA. *Well!* No wonder he was in such a state. *Your* Piglet!

POOH. So if you'd kindly give him back—

KANGA. I'll do no such thing! What an idea. The poor little thing is having proper care for the first time in its life. Now move aside!

POOH. Gr-r-r.

KANGA. Out of the way—*(Advances to just in front of POOH.)*

POOH. Gr-r-r-!

KANGA. What was that?

POOH *(giving it all he has)*. GR-R-R-R!!!

KANGA *(agitated, backing away from him toward DLC)*. Oh, dear—oh, *dear!*

POOH *(advancing proudly, a sort of gorilla fashion)*. Gr-rr-rr-r— *(But he has become rather hoarse, and ends up with a coughing sound.)* Ug-ugh!

KANGA *(very agitated, backing away toward L)*. Now keep away from us! Don't you come near us! *(Continues to hold onto PIGLET and ROO.)*

ROO *(awed by POOH)*. Oo-o-oh!

POOH. Frightening, isn't it?

KANGA. Dreadful. *Simply* dreadful!

POOH *(remembering to snarl)*. Gr-r-row-w-w—*(Again he coughs slightly.)*

KANGA. I've never heard anything like it.

POOH *(advancing again)*. And I'll keep it up until you let Piglet go.

KANGA *(shaking a finger at him, letting go of ROO)*. You'll keep it up until you do something about it. That's the worst cold I've ever seen—

POOH *(stopping)*. Cold?

KANGA. Down in your chest, too. *(This time she advances, still shaking her finger at him.)* Take my advice—go *straight* to bed!

POOH. I do *not* have a cold. *(But his voice breaks.)*

KANGA *(continuing to advance DRC, still clutching PIG-LET)*. And I suppose you make dreadful noises like that just for fun? Or to frighten us? Ha, ha! *(POOH makes a strangled sound in his throat. KANGA fumbles for something in her pocket.)* If you've any sense at all, which you probably haven't—you'll take some of this cough medicine. *(She thrusts a bottle at him, and he jumps at the sight of it.)* One spoonful every half hour.

POOH. No, thank you!

ROO *(gleefully)*. Drink it all! It tastes like poison! *(POOH retreats to R, shuddering slightly.)*

KANGA *(sighing)*. Foolish bear…*(Puts the bottle back.)* But we can't help those who won't help themselves. *(Takes ROO's hand.)* Come, Roo and Piglet. We'll finish our walk. Then a bath—and a little nap—*(ROO crosses to her and takes hold of her hand, but with great reluctance.)*

POOH. Wait—wait a minute—

KANGA *(hustling them out DR)*. Chin up, Piglet. *(Gives him a little jerk.)* One, two—*(Voice fades after they go out.)* One, two—*(POOH takes a feeble step or two DR in their direction, then stands dejectedly still. He is shaken by an involuntary cough, and stares ahead, much frightened, clutching his chest.)*

POOH. Owl! Eeyore!

(After a moment's pause, OWL and EEYORE come creeping onstage from DR, peering back over their shoulders.)

OWL. What happened?

EEYORE. Was she frightened?

POOH *(crossing to C)*. I don't feel very well. It's gone to my chest...*(EEYORE and OWL still DR exchange puzzled looks.)*

OWL *(severely, to POOH)*. Apparently Kanga walked off with Piglet while you just stood there. *(POOH hangs his head in shame.)*

EEYORE *(moving to DRC)*. Perhaps it all happens for the best, and it's useless to struggle...

POOH *(turning to face them)*. Why can't we all go after them? If we *all* surrounded her—

OWL. I don't think much of that idea.

POOH. But you should have *seen* Piglet. He's turned a different color—and there's a bow tied around his neck! It can't go on. Piglet is *miserable!*

EEYORE. *I'm* miserable. And it goes on—and on—

POOH. If we were to take action—all of us, *together*—

OWL. I'd love to, old fellow. But I have a previous engagement.

EEYORE *(crossing to beside OWL, DR)*. So have I.

OWL *(helpfully)*. Why don't you ask Rabbit?

POOH. Rabbit?

OWL. He said a good deal about taking action.

POOH. Where will I find him?

OWL. He's probably at home. Try knocking. *(OWL and EEYORE go out DL.)*

POOH. It's a good idea. Rabbit does things. *(Hesitates.)* Anyway, he says he does things. *(POOH crosses to LC and knocks on tree. After a moment's wait for an answer, he knocks again and calls.)* Rabbit?

(RABBIT comes on stage, from either UR or UL, in his house which is the entire upper third of the stage—cautiously and with an alarmed expression on his face. He stands URC.)

POOH. Is anybody home? *(RABBIT shakes his head "no" but makes no sound. POOH puts a paw to his ear.)* What I said was, "Is anybody home?"

RABBIT *(looking desperately around, in a shrill, disguised tone)*. No!

POOH. Bother! *(Turns toward DC and thinks a minute, then over his shoulder.)* Isn't there anybody at all?

RABBIT *(same tone)*. Nobody!

POOH *(thoughtfully, to himself)*. There must be somebody there—because somebody said "nobody"—*(Calls again.)* Hello. Could you kindly tell me where Rabbit is?

RABBIT. He's gone to see his friend, Pooh Bear.

POOH. Oh. *(Turns back.)* But this is me! Pooh.

RABBIT. Oh, well, then—come in. *(Nervously retreats to UR. As POOH struggles through the small opening, into RABBIT's house, RABBIT continues.)* It *is* you. I'm glad.

POOH *(standing UC)*. Who did you think it was?

RABBIT. Well, you know how it is lately—you can't be too careful—can't have just anybody coming in...

POOH. Piglet's got to be rescued from Kanga. And I can't seem to do it alone. So if you'll come with me—

RABBIT. Right now?

POOH. You *do* like to take action, don't you?

RABBIT. Certainly!

POOH. Owl and Eeyore won't do anything. They're afraid of her—

RABBIT *(contemptuously)*. A-ha!

POOH. Not like *you*—

RABBIT. Not at all!

POOH. So let's go right now. *(Starts for Rabbit Hole entrance.)*

RABBIT *(hesitating, trying wildly to think of something).* Ah—Pooh?

POOH *(turning back to reprove him for not coming at once).* We don't want to waste time—

RABBIT. Wait a moment. I nearly forgot—

POOH. What?

RABBIT *(taking a step toward cupboard URC).* Lunch. *(POOH pauses—this word registers.)*

POOH *(shaking himself firmly).* No time for that—

RABBIT *(restraining him).* Imagine my forgetting to eat lunch. Won't you join me?

POOH. No, no!

RABBIT *(turning around, reaching for a pot).* Fancy—I didn't know I had all this honey. *(Looks inside.)*

POOH. But Piglet—

RABBIT. Nearly a full pot, wouldn't you say? *(Holds it out under POOH's nose.)*

POOH. Piglet—*(Catches the scent, almost sways toward the pot and away from the door.)* Honey—

RABBIT *(going a step closer to POOH).* Quite full, I'd say...

POOH. Honey...

RABBIT *(holding the pot to POOH).* Help yourself. Or would you prefer marmalade? *(Produces a pot of this from top of cupboard. POOH eyes the honey, then the marmalade.)*

POOH *(bursting out after an internal struggle).* Both! *(Sits in chair, takes a spoon from his pocket and begins to eat furiously.)*

RABBIT *(putting the marmalade beside him).* Here we are.

POOH *(between mouthfuls).* I really shouldn't—*(Gulp.)*—take the time—*(Gulp.)*—must rescue Piglet—

RABBIT. One does better at rescuing after a bite to eat.

POOH (*eating voraciously, putting down empty honey pot and starting on the marmalade*). Much better...

RABBIT. One needs strength.

POOH (*setting down the empty marmalade pot beside the empty honey pot*). I *do* feel stronger! And now—

RABBIT. Have some more?

POOH (*looking into the pots*). There isn't any more.

RABBIT. I have another, someplace—

(*ROO runs onstage from DR, looking over his shoulder.*)

POOH. No, thank you—

RABBIT (*producing another pot from cupboard*). Here it is.

POOH. I really couldn't...(*ROO has been looking around the stage for a place to hide.*)

RABBIT (*waving the opened pot under POOH's nose*). Just a nibble?

KANGA'S VOICE (*calling anxiously from off DR*). Roo! Roo—where *are* you? (*ROO darts around frantically.*)

POOH (*weakening*). Perhaps just—a—very—tiny—(*Grabs the pot and digs in.*)

KANGA'S VOICE. Roo—come back here this minute! Do you hear me? (*A wrathful tone.*) Wait till I catch you, you naughty thing—(*ROO spots RABBIT's house, finds the doorway, and dives in.*)

RABBIT (*startled at the sudden arrival, retreating to UR*). Help!

POOH. Why, it's Roo!

ROO. Hello.

RABBIT. It can't be—not Kanga's Roo!

(KANGA enters from DR, searching wildly, and dragging PIGLET.)

KANGA. Roo—Roo-oo-oo! *(Her tone changes from anger to concern.)* Oh, dear, is the little thing lost? Oh, dear *me*— *(Pauses DLC.)*

ROO *(as POOH and RABBIT listen).* Sh-h-h!

RABBIT *(UR).* Playing hide-and-seek, perhaps? *(ROO nods with great vigor.)*

ROO *(URC).* Sh-h-h!

KANGA *(quite desperate).* Oh, the poor baby—what will become of him! *(To PIGLET.)* We *must* find him!

PIGLET. Yes, we must.

KANGA. The things that might happen—

PIGLET. I have an idea.

KANGA. What is it?

PIGLET. Why don't you look for Roo over there—*(Points in one direction.)*—and I'll look for him over *there. (Points in the opposite direction.)*

KANGA. And have you getting lost, too? *(Clutches PIGLET closer to her side, as he makes a face.)* My goodness, no. I wouldn't dare let you out of my sight—not for a minute! *(Drags him off again, calling:)* Roo—Roo, my precious! *(They go out DL.)*

ROO. I'm not really lost. I ran away.

POOH. You did?

ROO. I've always wanted to run away.

RABBIT. Youth will be youth.

ROO *(delightedly).* Look! I'm all dirty! And I have germs *all over* me! *(RABBIT and POOH look puzzled.)*

RABBIT *(feeling he must do something).* How about a piece of candy?

ROO *(eagerly). Candy!*

RABBIT *(offering him a box from the cupboard)*. Have one.

ROO. I'm never supposed to eat candy before supper! *(Takes one.)* Can I have more?

RABBIT. Of course.

ROO *(going at the candy with energy)*. This is fun. I like it here! *(As ROO munches the candy delightedly, POOH notices RABBIT looking very sober. POOH struggles from his chair with difficulty because of his weight [he may have stuffed a small pillow into his shirt if this can be managed unobtrusively].)*

POOH *(to RABBIT)*. Why are you frowning like that?

RABBIT. Sooner or later, she's going to find out.

POOH. Kanga?

RABBIT. And there's bound to be a—*(Tremulous tone.)*—disturbance.

ROO. It's all gone!

RABBIT *(absently handing him another box)*. Have some more. *(ROO grabs, and RABBIT turns back to POOH.)* "Where have you been?" she'll ask—"At Rabbit's house," he'll answer—*(RABBIT shudders.)*

POOH. On the other hand, she'll be glad to see him.

RABBIT. Oh, yes.

POOH *(crossing to UR)*. She thinks he's lost. And losing one's offspring causes a good bit of worry—

RABBIT *(flinging up his paws)*. I've been through it myself. Perfect agony!

POOH. When he *does* turn up safe and sound—won't she be happy?

RABBIT. Terribly happy!

POOH *(thoughtfully)*. Do you suppose she might offer a reward—to somebody who brought Roo home safe and sound—

RABBIT. She might very well—

POOH. And if that somebody were *me*—and I could have a reward—that reward might be—

RABBIT. Piglet!

POOH *(quietly triumphant)*. Piglet.

ROO *(looking up at them suspiciously)*. Who said anything about bringing me home?

POOH. After all, sooner or later—

ROO. I don't *want* to go home!

RABBIT. I'm glad to have you come and visit, of course. But your mother—think how she misses you—

ROO. She has Piglet—she won't miss me so much. She has to give him so many *baths! (POOH's and RABBIT's faces darken.)* And that medicine—

POOH. What medicine?

ROO. You should have seen it. She had to try five spoonfuls before she got him to swallow it. *(POOH and RABBIT shudder.)* And then he *said* something—

RABBIT. What? *(ROO crosses, whispers something to RABBIT, who looks startled.)*

ROO. So then she had to wash out his mouth with *soap—* *(ROO crosses to chair and sits.)* So I don't have to go home.

POOH *(crossing to his side)*. Come, Roo.

ROO. But—

POOH. I hate to do it, but you're going home.

ROO. I am not! *(Sits firmly and rocks chair.)*

RABBIT *(crossing to ROO, trying a more diplomatic approach)*. Go ahead, Pooh—we'll follow. Hurry! *(POOH prepares to go out the doorway LC.)*

POOH. There's not a moment to lose—*(Stops, head and shoulders out of the doorway.)*—to—oof!

RABBIT. What's the matter?

POOH *(trying to get through)*. Nothing...

RABBIT *(crossing to L where he can push).* Hurry up. You're blocking the door. *(POOH grunts with the struggle.)* You're not stuck? *(POOH makes a frantic effort, with no result.)*

ROO. He *is* stuck!

RABBIT *(puts his paw to his forehead).* But we can't get out—

ROO *(overjoyed).* We *can't?* *(He leaps up and cavorts and dances URC and UR while RABBIT tries frantically to push POOH through the doorway.)* Whee! I don't have to go home! *(He bounces up and down.)* Hurrah! *(RABBIT gives up.)*

POOH. Bother!

ROO *(loud and shrill).* Wheeeeee!

POOH *(calling out in an irritated tone).* It all comes of not having front doors big enough.

RABBIT. It all comes—*(Crosses and looks sadly into the empty pots of honey.)*—of eating too much!

(KANGA enters from DL, still dragging PIGLET, who looks a little frazzled. KANGA looks anxiously around.)

ROO *(continuing his squeals of ecstasy).* Whee-ee—

POOH *(as he sees KANGA).* Sh-h-h!

KANGA *(from DL).* I heard him. I'm sure I heard him. Roo? Roo, dear? *(ROO, having grabbed another piece of candy, is silent as he eats it.)*

PIGLET. I did, too. A squealing sound.

KANGA. Roo? Where are you?

PIGLET *(leading the way to RABBIT's house LC).* It seemed to be coming from Rabbit's—*(Takes a look at POOH, uncomprehendingly.)*—Rabbit's house...

KANGA. Roo, are you in there?

POOH (*quickly*). No.

KANGA. What are you doing in the doorway?

POOH (*desperately, assuming an appropriate pose*). Oh, rest-
ing—and thinking—

ROO (*at URC, finished with the candy, demanding more from
RABBIT*). Isn't there any more? (*RABBIT has been listening nervously to what goes on outside.*)

RABBIT. Sh—hhh—

ROO. I want more! *More!* M—(*RABBIT cuts it off by putting
his paw over ROO's mouth.*)

KANGA (*frantically*). It's Roo! He *is* in there. Roo. Roo? (*To
POOH.*) Get out of the way, you absurd creature—

POOH. Well, you see—

KANGA (*interrupting*). Hurry up!

POOH. That is to say—

PIGLET. He's stuck.

KANGA. *What?* You can't be stuck in a doorway, and my
Roo inside! (*Grabs one of POOH's ears and tugs on it.*)
My precious—my baby—(*She is quite hysterical now.*)

POOH. Oh, help!

RABBIT (*grabbing POOH's hind feet*). I'll try to pull you
back! (*KANGA lets go of PIGLET, who remains spell-
bound. She grabs POOH's forepaws and starts to pull.*)

KANGA (*wildly*). We'll see about this—(*She pulls one way,
RABBIT pulls the other.*)

POOH (*roaring*). Let me go-o-o-o!

RABBIT (*calling*). I'm trying to get you in—somehow—

KANGA. You wretched bear, I'll get you out—

POOH. But not—not *both!* (*RABBIT gives up, exhausted.
KANGA pulls the first thing she can find—a washrag—out
of her pocket and starts whacking POOH over the head
with it. She is completely unstrung.*)

KANGA. You're just doing this to be stubborn!

POOH *(covering his head, trying to protest).* No—no—
(Lights start down.)

KANGA *(continuing to whack at him wildly).* My Roo in that
dreadful place—and you won't let him out—nasty, stubborn thing! *(Still whacking.)* Take that—and that—and
that! *(Lights go down.)*

*(CHRISTOPHER ROBIN enters in dark and sits on has-
sock DR. Spot up. This time he is holding the teddy bear
tightly, with an anxious expression on his face.)*

VOICE *(narrator, offstage).* And there they were—Rabbit and
Roo trapped inside Rabbit's house, Pooh stuck in the doorway, Kanga too upset to realize it was no use whacking
him over the head with a washrag—*(The tone changes.)*
My word.

CHRISTOPHER ROBIN. Go on—

VOICE. I didn't realize—it's past your bedtime.

CHRISTOPHER ROBIN. Oh, *please*—

VOICE. Shall we finish another time?

CHRISTOPHER ROBIN. But we can't *possibly* sleep—not
unless you finish the story—

VOICE *(ominously).* Suppose it has a bad ending?

CHRISTOPHER ROBIN *(hadn't thought of this possibility).*
It couldn't—everything always comes out all right—

VOICE. I wonder what Eeyore would say to that.

CHRISTOPHER ROBIN *(alarmed).* *Doesn't* it? I mean,
*some*how Pooh got out of Rabbit's doorway—he'd get
thinner and thinner, and then—

VOICE *(a touch of asperity).* Who is telling this story?

CHRISTOPHER ROBIN. Oh! I'm truly sorry.

VOICE. As a matter of fact, he did get thinner. But it took
time.

CHRISTOPHER ROBIN. And Kanga? Excuse me—

VOICE. She calmed down a good bit when Rabbit promised to take very good care of Roo. He had a box of oatmeal— and that made Kanga feel *much* better. Of course, Rabbit forgot to mention that the box was empty...After about a week, Pooh was thin enough to be pulled out. It was a great day—

CHRISTOPHER ROBIN. I should think so!

VOICE. It was his birthday, too...MOST OF RABBIT'S FRIENDS HAD COME 'ROUND, HOPING THERE'D BE A PARTY. They all helped pull...*(The capitalized speech may be used if extras are available and have been used in the earlier scenes. Otherwise, the VOICE should say, "It was his birthday, too. Everyone was there— Eeyore, Owl, and all the others.")*

(CHRISTOPHER ROBIN goes out R. Lights up on another part of the forest, a little to the "west" of Rabbit's house. The same trees DR and DL frame the stage, and there is a third tree against the back wall ULC. A long line, consisting of OWL, EEYORE, and ANIMALS 1, 2, 3 and 4, extends from offstage DR, diagonally back toward UL. Each is pulling at the waist of the one in front of him. The front person in line, who is offstage, has hold of POOH and is pulling him out of the rabbit hole. NOTE: Any and all extra characters used in the flight across the stage at the end of Act One may be used instead of OWL, EEYORE, and ANIMALS 1, 2, 3 and 4.)

VOICE. A long line of them—they waited for the signal.

ANIMAL *(shouting signal, offstage)*. One—two—three—

VOICE. Then pulled—*(The ANIMALS strain backward, pulling like anything.)* And, finally—(A loud pop is heard. One*

*by one, the ANIMALS fall over backward, with the release
of POOH. Cries of "Hurrah"— "We did it"— "He's out"—
are ad libbed by the young ANIMALS.)*

OWL *(looking severe, from a position C)*. Hush. Hush! *(They
calm down.)* Not so much noise. *(The ANIMALS group
themselves in a semicircle from UC to DLC, facing OWL.)*

ANIMAL 1. Why?

ANIMAL 2. We're celebrating!

ANIMAL 3. After all, we pulled Pooh out—

ANIMAL 4. And it's his birthday, too!

ANIMAL 3. Yes!

ANIMAL 2. Isn't there going to be a party?

OWL. Sh-h-h! This is no time for parties and celebrations.
Now run along! *(Points offstage DR. ANIMALS reluctantly
go out DR, leaving only OWL on stage.)*

(POOH enters past them, looking weak and thin.)

POOH *(all business, from RC)*. She doesn't know?

OWL. Not yet.

POOH. Good. Rabbit is taking Roo to a safe place.

OWL. A good distance away? *(POOH nods.)* I expect you
know the procedure...*(POOH looks puzzled. OWL ex-
plains.)* What to do...

POOH *(as if repeating a lesson)*. I go to Kanga. *(Shudders.)*

OWL *(with asperity)*. You *confront* Kanga—

POOH. She'll naturally ask where Baby Roo is—

OWL. Yes, yes—

POOH. And I say, "A-ha."

OWL *(nodding with satisfaction)*. *That* will give her the idea.

POOH. How? After all, "A-ha" could mean almost anything.

OWL. Pooh, you haven't any brain. "A-ha" means that Baby Roo is hidden in a secret place, and we'll tell her where it is if she'll let Piglet go.

POOH. "A-ha." *(Dubiously.)* It *does?*

OWL *(looking off DR in the direction of RABBIT's house)*. I hope Rabbit gets his part right. Can he manage Roo?

POOH *(nodding)*. They got on beautifully. Roo enjoyed his visit *very* much.

OWL *(a touch of annoyance)*. Rabbit ought to know how to amuse youngsters.

POOH *(sincere enthusiasm for RABBIT's talent)*. Oh, yes! He gave him peppermints—and gumdrops—and sometimes licorice—

OWL. Plenty of experience, Rabbit's had.

POOH. Roo liked jelly beans the best. *(Sighs.)* It's a shame he has to go home at all.

OWL. No doubt he'll make quite a fuss.

(ROO enters from DR, followed by RABBIT. ROO is in bad shape. His expression is of one green with an upset stomach.)

POOH. If it weren't for Piglet—

ROO *(clutches his stomach in agony)*. Oo-o-o-o-ooh! *(He wanders around, making a circuit of the stage and stopping the second time he reaches DLC.)*

POOH. Why, Roo!

OWL. What are you doing here?

RABBIT. I can't do a thing with him.

ROO. Ooh-oh-oh-oh-oooo—

RABBIT. He wants to go home.

POOH. But he can't, not *yet*—

OWL *(to RABBIT)*. Think of *something!*

RABBIT (*crossing to ROO, holding out a little bag*). Here, little fellow—the last bag of jelly beans—

ROO (*taking one look and sitting down weakly on the floor*). Na-a-ooo-o-ow!

RABBIT (*turning to OTHERS*). I simply don't understand! (*To ROO.*) Now tell Uncle Rabbit—what *would* you like?

ROO (*a weak, pathetic tone*). Some—some castor oil—

OWL (*motioning to RABBIT*). That's enough. You'd better hustle him off right away—

ROO. I want to go home! (*RABBIT reaches for him, but ROO gets up and plunges off DL, wailing in agony.*) I want to be put to bed! (*Going out.*) I want my mama-a-a-a...(*ALL watch his exit. POOH and OWL turn and look at RABBIT somewhat reproachfully. RABBIT finally turns to face them, shrugs and makes a helpless gesture with his paws.*)

RABBIT. Well—that's that.

OWL. I don't like to mention it—but in view of your family experience, one would hope you'd do a *little* better—

RABBIT. I can't help it. He got sick!

POOH. I wonder why. Did he eat anything strange?

RABBIT (*pacing up and down from ULC to DLC*). Anything besides peppermint—jelly beans—gumdrops—licorice? (*Thinks it over.*) Nothing else.

POOH. I don't understand it.

OWL. But there it is—

POOH (*hollow tone*). There it is. (*Crosses to DR.*)

RABBIT. I suppose Piglet will have to stay with Kanga forever.

OWL. Which is a long time.

POOH. It will *seem* long—to Piglet—

(*ALL stare dolefully into different directions of space as EEYORE comes in from DR.*)

EEYORE *(an unaccountably cheerful manner)*. Good morning, Owl—and Rabbit—*and* Pooh—

RABBIT. *Good* morning?

POOH *(gazing DR)*. I don't think it's a good morning—

OWL. Quite the opposite. *(Looks off DL, while RABBIT looks
at his feet.)*

EEYORE *(RC)*. Pooh Bear—I've come to wish you a happy
birthday.

POOH *(absently, not looking at him)*. It is?

EEYORE *(very proud of himself)*. I'd been so afraid I'd forget all about it. But I didn't.

POOH *(turning to EEYORE)*. What?

EEYORE. Forget your birthday.

POOH. Oh.

EEYORE *(looking at ALL with some annoyance)*. What's everyone so *gloomy* about? If there's one thing I can't bear,
it's a gloomy attitude...

POOH. I'm sorry, Eeyore. *(OWL begins to pace back and
forth between C and L.)*

EEYORE. Now my entire day is ruined. *(With the usual
sigh.)* But so it goes—

POOH *(to himself, very sadly)*. My birthday. *(Faces DC.)*

RABBIT. What a shame you can't have a party.

POOH. Not without Piglet.

RABBIT. He was so fond of parties—

POOH. With refreshments—and songs—and games—

EEYORE. "Here-we-go-'round-the-mulberry-bush—"

POOH *(practically in tears)*. "London Bridge" was his favorite.

RABBIT. All because Kanga must have someone to put in
her bathtub!

OWL *(echoing)*. Yes, she must have someone...

POOH. Hm-m-m...*(Getting an idea.)* I suppose—anyone
would do...

EEYORE. I can't help wondering why it wasn't me. I always get the dirty end of things.

POOH *(wrapped in his own train of thought, exclaiming suddenly)*. Yes! It's the—the pro—*(Fumbles with the word.)*—cedure.

OWL. Whatever are you talking about?

POOH. The Thing To Do.

RABBIT. What is?

POOH *(advancing to DC)*. If *any*one can—*(Gulps.)*—take baths, and all that—well, anyone could offer—to take Piglet's place.

OWL. But who—

POOH *(bravely)*. *I* will. *(Stunned silence.)*

EEYORE *(finally, shaking his head)*. I believe I'm hearing things. I thought Pooh said—

RABBIT. He did. *(POOH stands looking upward in an exalted manner. He is oblivious for the moment. The OTHERS go into a brief huddle URC, whispering to each other. Finally OWL steps over to POOH.)*

OWL. Ahem...Pooh, have you considered this carefully? We feel terrible about Piglet, and friendship is all very well—

RABBIT. But think of it! Baths—and soap—and oatmeal—

EEYORE. Life isn't *much* around here, but won't you miss it?

POOH *(moving to LC, turning to them, nodding soberly)*. I shall. I'll miss a great many things—*(Reminiscent sigh.)*—a peaceful walk in the forest—humming, or just thinking—visiting a friend—now and then having a little something—It's hard to give it all up. A pleasant sort of life—*(Sadly shakes his head.)*—but not a very useful life—*(ALL are very much moved.)*

EEYORE. Just—*(A sob.)*—happy—

POOH *(ready to go)*. Farewell!

RABBIT. Not now—not on your *birthday!*

OWL. It's highly improper to give up everything on your birthday!

POOH. But—

OWL *(interrupting)*. It wouldn't *look* right.

(KANGA enters from DL, storming along and pulling PIG-LET by the hand, of course.)

KANGA. So—*there* you are! *(POOH backs up a few steps toward the OTHERS at URC.)*

POOH, OWL, EEYORE and RABBIT. Kanga! *(She pauses.)*

KANGA *(from LC)*. Rabbit—*(Marches in his direction.)* Rabbit, *indeed!* I'm going to give you a piece of my mind! *(But RABBIT doesn't want it. He walks, with the OTHERS, at a faster and faster pace, till they are running the last few steps offstage DR. POOH starts to run, also, but turns back as he reaches DR. KANGA advances to C and calls after them.)* Little Roo has *never* been in such a condition. *(She sees it is no use pursuing them.)*

PIGLET *(to POOH, in a strange, faraway voice)*. Hello, Pooh...

POOH. Hello, Piglet. I suppose you feel terribly angry at me—

PIGLET. No—I don't—

POOH. Really?

PIGLET *(a numb tone)*. I don't seem to feel *anything*...not anymore—

POOH *(as KANGA turns to lead PIGLET away DL)*. Oh, *Piglet! (Beside himself.)* Birthday or no birthday—I can't stand it any longer—*(He runs around between KANGA and DL.)*

KANGA. What do *you* want?

POOH. I'm going with you!

KANGA *(with immense disgust)*. *You?* You most certainly are not!

POOH. Oh, dear me—

KANGA. Nasty, dirty creature! Come, Piglet.

POOH *(stopping her)*. Wait! You're right. I *am* dirty—

KANGA. At least you admit it.

POOH. Maybe you don't know how *very* dirty—*(He holds out his paws.)*

KANGA *(looking at them)*. Tsk, tsk—*(Takes another look, and becomes interested.)* Heavens!

POOH. Aren't they terrible? And just see—*(Cups an ear, leaning over so she can inspect it.)*

KANGA *(becoming more interested)*. My *word*—

POOH. And the teeth—*(Opens his mouth.)* Ah-h-h—

KANGA *(jumping back, so dreadful is this sight)*. Ee-e-e-e!

POOH. They've never been brushed.

KANGA *(fascinated)*. *Never?*

POOH. And my fur—full of burrs, and snarls—

KANGA *(really with him now)*. A good combing! Wouldn't I love to go over you with a steel comb—

POOH. You would?

KANGA. And then a bath—

POOH *(hollow voice)*. Yes. A bath. When shall we begin?

KANGA. What?

POOH. Well, you just said—

KANGA. I'd love to. But what with Roo feeling sick—and I can't neglect Piglet—

POOH. Oh, Piglet could go home. You'd have *me*.

KANGA *(frowning)*. Piglet—go home? *(POOH nods, leaning forward with suspense.)* But I'm fond of Piglet. I doubt if I could get very fond of you. *(POOH cups his ear again, temptingly. KANGA's eyes light up again.)* I can't resist. Such a challenge—I've never seen *anything* so dirty!

POOH *(modestly)*. Thank you.

KANGA. Piglet, you'll have to be brave—*(PIGLET, C, looks up from his daze, startled a bit.)* From now on, you'll have to take care of yourself. *(Lets go of his hand. PIGLET doesn't seem to understand what's happening.)* But remember, dear—whenever you need a bath, come over and we'll manage, somehow—*(Takes POOH's hand.)*

POOH *(waving)*. Good-bye, Piglet. *(KANGA tugs at him toward DL. He takes a last look in the other direction, then pulls himself together and bravely marches off DL with KANGA.)*

(PIGLET, left alone, begins to come to his senses. He shakes himself, pinches himself, looks around, and smiles, then grabs off the bow about his neck. He begins to skip around as the OTHERS enter from DR—first OWL, then RABBIT, EEYORE and ANIMALS 1, 2, 3 and 4. ALL pause in wonder between RC and DR, watching PIGLET cavort.)

RABBIT *(pointing at PIGLET)*. Look—he's done it! *(PIGLET lies on the ground LC and rolls over a few times.)*

OWL. Whoever would have thought—

EEYORE *(to PIGLET, approvingly)*. That's right, Piglet—getting back your old color again...

ANIMAL 1 *(crossing cautiously to DL, peering after POOH and KANGA)*. I can *see* them!

ANIMAL 2 *(joining ANIMAL 1 DL)*. Have they gotten to Kanga's house?

ANIMAL 1. Yes!

ANIMAL 3 (joining them). Look, she's putting water in the tub.

RABBIT. Already?

ANIMAL 4 *(also joining OTHERS DL)*. Ooooh—there's smoke coming out of the water!

ANIMAL 3. Steam, silly!

ANIMAL 1. He's saying something to Kanga!

PIGLET *(knowingly, as he sits on the floor LC)*. He's telling her the water is too hot.

ANIMAL 1. Now she's saying something to Pooh—

PIGLET *(looking DC)*. Telling him it's all his imagination.

ANIMAL 1. Oh, oh—he's getting in—*(OBSERVERS stare in excited horror. At the moment when POOH presumably gets in, it's too much—ALL turn their heads or avert their eyes in horror. Silence.)*

OWL *(advancing to RC, finally, in an uncomfortable tone)*. Of course, Pooh has no one but himself to blame.

EEYORE. That's some consolation.

RABBIT. When one has bad habits—like overeating—

OWL. And *very* little brain—

EEYORE. Hardly any at all.

ANIMAL 1 *(who has taken another peek)*. She's scrubbing him—with a great big brush! *(ANIMALS 2, 3, and 4 DL go back to watching the procedure.)*

RABBIT. Of course, he *did* have ideas.

OWL. Interesting ideas.

EEYORE. Rather good company, too...*(PIGLET is suddenly overwhelmed at what has happened.)*

PIGLET. He was my best friend—*(He sprawls on the floor to sob with his head in his arms.)*

RABBIT. There, there, Piglet.

OWL. Baths don't last forever.

PIGLET *(sitting up, drying his eyes)*. But afterward comes—comes the Strengthening Medicine—*(They shake their heads sadly.)*

RABBIT. Does it taste bad?

PIGLET. A big spoonful—*horrible*—ugh!
ANIMAL 1. Oh—look out! *(Turns and starts to run to DR.)*
EEYORE. What's the matter?
ANIMAL 2 *(also running to DR)*. She's coming—
ANIMAL 3. Run!

(ALL on stage cluster DR as POOH dashes in DL. He is clutching a large bath towel around his middle. If possible, handfuls of soap suds are sticking to him. KANGA runs in DL, chasing him with a bottle and teaspoon.)

POOH. Oh, no—not that—
KANGA *(from L)*. Come here—*(Very sharply.)* Pooh! *(POOH halts in the middle of the stage.)* You haven't tasted it yet. How do you know you won't like it?
POOH. Just—one spoonful?
KANGA. One. *(She pours and advances to C to administer it.)*
POOH. All right. *(Opens his mouth, and she pops it in—as there is a horrified gasp from the crowd of ANIMALS. POOH swallows. Then he begins to react. There is much whispering among the OBSERVERS. POOH's expression of distaste turns blank. He opens his eyes very wide, then begins to smile in a surprised fashion.)* A strange thing—*(He looks at the bottle.)*—it tastes like—honey!
KANGA. Naturally! Honey is one of the ingredients.
POOH. It is?
KANGA. You see, honey is very strengthening.
POOH. *I've* always thought so! *(Reaches for bottle with both paws.)* Could I please have another—
KANGA *(handing it to him, rather pleased)*. It's *good* for you!
POOH *(after one more spoonful)*. An unusual sort of honey—but just the same—*(He drinks it out of the bottle, gulping it down.)*

KANGA. What are you doing? *(Worried.)* You needn't drink it *all. (As he keeps on.)* Think of Baby Roo—*he* needs to be strengthened, too. Give me that *bottle!*

POOH *(handing it back, empty).* Ah-h-h.

KANGA *(furious).* Empty!

POOH. I don't suppose you have any—more?

KANGA. No! *(Steps away from him, toward DL).* At any rate, *you're* not going to have any more. *(POOH follows, KANGA waves him back.)* Stay where you are!

POOH *(from DLC).* Aren't I supposed to go with you?

KANGA. I'm sorry. I'd like to take care of you—*(Waves her arm around, to indicate the OTHERS.)*—and all the rest of them—*(She looks at the bottle.)*—but I have Roo to think of. I can't do *everything. (Turns and goes off with righteous indignation, muttering.)* A *whole* bottle—my word, indeed—*(Goes out DL.)*

POOH *(staring after her).* Bother.

RABBIT *(as ALL begin to come forward several steps).* Bother?

POOH *(turning to face them).* Until I tasted that medicine, I didn't realize how hungry I was...

OWL. Pooh, it didn't seem possible that your appetite could be useful.

POOH. It is? *(Puzzled.)* How?

OWL *(shaking his head). Very* little brain. But you got rid of Kanga. You saved your friend, Piglet. And everything can be the way it was again—all because of Pooh! *(ALL cheer, shouting "Hooray for Pooh!" etc.)*

(CHRISTOPHER ROBIN enters from DL, pulling a wagon on which is a cake with candles on it, a present, and some assorted candy.)

CHRISTOPHER ROBIN. Here we are. Surprise! *(Pulls wagon to C.)*

PIGLET. Christopher Robin!

CHRISTOPHER ROBIN. Happy Birthday, Pooh! *(Indicates wagon.)*

RABBIT *(as he and OTHERS cluster around wagon)*. Look— a birthday cake!

EEYORE. —with candles—

PIGLET. And all sorts of refreshments!

CHRISTOPHER ROBIN *(to POOH)*. And here's a present— because you sacrificed yourself for your friend—because you're such a good bear after all. *(Hands POOH a package, ALL cheer again.)* Many happy returns...

POOH. Thank you!

CHRISTOPHER ROBIN. I didn't know what you wanted, so I just got you something useful—*(As he speaks, POOH unwraps a large pot with "Honey" written on it in large letters.)*

POOH *(overwhelmed)*. I don't know what to say.

OWL. In that case, I suggest you pass the refreshments.

CHRISTOPHER ROBIN. A good idea! *(POOH takes a basket of candy—the sort that is individually wrapped—and starts passing them out. The young ANIMALS clamor "Me!" "Don't forget me!" etc.)*

POOH *(anxiously, to CHRISTOPHER ROBIN)*. Is there enough?

CHRISTOPHER ROBIN. Plenty—for everybody!

POOH *(grinning)*. Well, in that case—I want everyone to have some—*(He comes up to the footlights and begins tossing candy to the audience.)* A little something for everybody—*(As he comes to the end of the candy, he adds regretfully.)* There doesn't seem to be any more—*(Curtain starts falling.)* So this is the end.

CURTAIN—END

PRODUCTION NOTES

SETTING: A bare stage with neutral curtain or exterior backing, or a line of flats painted in a neutral color, along the upstage wall. DR, painted on a flat or on a piece of canvas and serving as a wing, is a tree. There is another tree DL. A third tree is URC. The location of this tree is changed before Act Two, and an aerial root is added to make a rabbit hole. Later, it is again moved, and the rabbit hole is removed.

While exits and entrances have been indicated in the appropriate spots, these, for the most part, are arbitrary and may be changed if necessary because of any particular staging problems.

The various stage movements given in the script are general in character. They will be influenced by the size of the stage and the amount of space available. Bear in mind that in a play of this sort, particularly on a stage that is almost bare, the action and movements must fill the stage. The absence of scenery and complicated properties must be replaced by movement of the characters. Where there is space, the characters will find that 3 steps are better than 2, and 4 better than 3.

CHARACTERS AND COSTUMES

CHRISTOPHER ROBIN: He should, if possible, be a little larger than the other characters in the play. He is dressed, however, as a young boy. No special costume is called for as long as he is neatly dressed in very young clothing.

NARRATOR'S VOICE: This may come from offstage and may be given either naturally or over a loud-speaker system. This part can also be easily handled on stage by a man or a woman. Any aunt or uncle type of adult will do, but since it is more of an uncle-type story, an uncle would be a better selection.

ANIMALS: All have purely representational make-up. They wear normal, inconspicuous clothing. Their heads are covered with close-fitting cloth caps which should be painted to represent the animals, with appropriate ears attached. Their facial make-up should carry out the animal theme wherever possible. If more elaborate or complete-animal costumes are desired, they will, of course, further dress the show. However, they are not necessary to an effective production of this work.

WINNIE-THE-POOH: He should have a cloth head covering with small bear ears, and a short tail.

PIGLET: He should be small and have a skin-colored cloth head covering with pig ears attached, and a short corkscrew tail. In Act Two he wears snowy white coveralls, and a bow is tied around his neck.

OWL: He should have owl ears and carefully painted cardboard wings extending from his shoulders to below his knees. The wings are operated by his arms, which should not show.

EEYORE: He should have donkey ears and a donkey tail.

KANGA: She should be as tall as possible and have a grey kangaroo-like cloth cap with ears, and a long thick tail. An apron with a pouch in it would be effective for Kanga.

ROO: Roo is a smaller version of Kanga.

RABBIT: He has white rabbit ears and a little "powder-puff" rabbit tail.

ANIMALS 1, 3 *and* 4: These animals are rabbits, but they may be easily changed (with minor line changes) to other animals, if so desired.

ANIMAL 2: He is a skunk and should have a white line running from the hair line on his forehead, over the top of his head, down the back of his neck, and running from the base to the tip of his tail.

Miscellaneous extra animals may be added, if available, in the places indicated in the script.

STAGE CHART

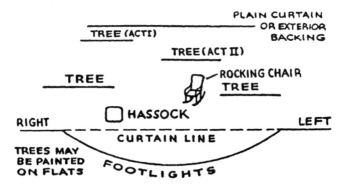

PROPERTIES

GENERAL: Nursery-size rocking chair; hassock; sign reading "Sanders"; a looped aerial root (entrance to Rabbit Hole); sign reading "Rabbit Hole"; cupboard containing two pots of honey, a pot of marmalade, and two boxes of candy.

CHRISTOPHER ROBIN: Teddy bear; large blue balloon; pop-gun; wagon containing birthday cake with candles on it, a wrapped gift (this is a large pot marked "Honey") and assorted candies in basket.

EEYORE: Two stalks of thistles.

KANGA: Round tin washtub containing a soapy washrag, bottle of iodine, bottle of cough medicine, another washrag, bottle and teaspoon.

ROO: Pitcher of water.

POOH: Spoon, bath towel.

RABBIT: Bag of jelly beans.

WHAT PEOPLE ARE SAYING about *Winnie-the-Pooh*...

"An excellent play for beginning actors. Perfect for a family oriented audience. Works very well with a small budget because of the limited set requirements and the basic animal costumes."
Alan Stevens, Durand High School, Durand, Ill.

"Delightful with appeal to both children and adults. We had many three-year-olds attend who loved it. Easily produced, too."
Harvey G. Cocks, Fort Wayne Youtheatre, Inc.,
Fort Wayne, Ind.

"Entertaining. Appropriate for a family audience. Humorous to both the old and young alike."   *Heather Steadham,*
Young Actors Guild, Fort Smith, Ark.

"*Winnie-the-Pooh* was a well-written script, a pleasure to perform. Our students (grades 1-6) found the script easy to read and the lines fun to memorize. It was exciting to bring Pooh to the stage."   *Ciara Stockeland, Third Street Acting Company,*
Fargo, N.D.

"*Winnie-the-Pooh* is a classic. The children in the audience get so excited, parents have to hold the children to keep them from going up on stage." "Over 60 little bodies froze in anticipation as Winnie-the-Pooh walked on stage. Forty some adults also had fun." "The children love Pooh. Three- and four-year-olds were glued to their seats..."   *Walter Williams,*
Master Arts Theatre, Grand Rapids, Mich.

"This is a delightful retelling of three of Pooh's greatest adventures! There is action, humor and some subtle lessons to be learned. We used five adults and twelve children. There are also some opportunities for audience participation!"   *Ron Solomon,*
Make It Up As We Go Productions, Pearland, Texas

DIRECTOR'S NOTES

DIRECTOR'S NOTES

DIRECTOR'S NOTES

DIRECTOR'S NOTES

DIRECTOR'S NOTES